OscilloTheorem

OscilloTheorem

Poems by Kenneth C. Fish Jr
Fishing Hole Books

© Kenneth C. Fish Jr

Published by
Fishing Hole Books
Napa, California

ISBN – 978-0-6152-0685-1

Acknowledgments

I'd like to thank Thomas Burke, and Jan Van Stavern, as well as the faculty and staff of the Archbishop Alemany Library of Dominican University for helping make this possible.

I also want to thank Jason Ezell and Liam Costernocht (a.k.a. Bxxx) who have been my semi-official sounding board during the writing of this book. Their time and willingness to put up with my irregular bombardments of words, worry and nonsense and their gentle encouragement helped me keep this book on track.

Many thanks to my buddy, Nayland Blake, for pushing me to "start another project."

Special thanks to Robbie Hayes whose love and support makes everything I do possible.

Content(s)

In the First Six Inches
Strain Displacements
It's Like When Men
Beautiful Sins
Remainders and Casualties
Of Surface and Substance
Tasks and Tick-marks
In Development
In Position
The Result
Balance
Second Nature
Contrarian
Evidence and Reasoning
To Be Expected
Theory and Law
Us or Them
In Beijing
Exchange
Tertiary
Interim
Null Set
Ether
Validation
In Simple Acceptance
Seam

Upheaval

Passing in the Fog

Turf

Magnetism

4.56am

When the Treetops Whistled

Opening of

In the Welling

Restoration

Of Opportunity

If Only Slight

Of Scrutiny and Hindsight

Man.1

Denouement

As if Gossamer

In the First Six Inches

waiting for the last passageway
the last chance to, from this grip
from the here and now, pass

waiting for the dreams to begin again
for the illuminations to, as if in a dream
land gently and for them to root roughly

and turn the soil, snouts darkening as
they go and lightening too, this earth, to the depth
of a man's hand, the tears, in torrents, racing

sorting the soils, and from it, analyzing
the dirt as it is unearthed, discovered
brought to the light where the birds

bickering on the dog-eared fence
wait for the witnesses to wander
wait for the backs to be turned

so they too, without interruption
or fear can sink deeply into
this fresh offering

Strain Displacements

as quickly there as they are gone
the metallic clack like a hammer hitting

at first benign, at first without definition
each instance lacking urgency as it comes
and goes
> *consider a rod and its initial length*
> *take into account the stretching of it*

nobody flinches, nobody moves at all
as if the unexpected weren't unexpected at
all

and then the sense of what is happening
the sudden realization that something is
happening
> *the strain measure*
> *a dimensionless ratio*

there is a building, a crescendo almost, like
momentum
involvement evolves into reaction, into what
do we do now

in this passing there is the chance of being
forgotten
there is hope in the prayers sent aloft, there

is potential
> *defined as the ratio of elongation*
> *with respect to the original length*

the open sky wrung clear by repercussion
thoughts are gathered and dashed, focused
and fragmented

in this, as the chaos blossoms, are we judge
or judgement
is the moment being defined as it unfolds or
do we define it
> *to track down the strain at each*

point
> *further refinement in the definition*

is   needed
with the opening of each door is there an
hierarchy established
chances grow and diminish, load and
unload, exploit the moment

as quickly there as they are gone
each an instance like a hammer hitting

It's Like When Men

the way hands fit together,
almost accidental interlacing
interlocking, a grip to fit a grip
in it, we share strength

the way when eyes meet there is a brief
reading
the glance, the stance
the quick steeling of oneself
sussed and sorted and on we go

the way patterns still exist,
in lives overlapping
overflowing
broken and reformed

what is mine is what is yours
the basic meaning of the moment
there is an exchange taking place
the way one has will over another.

Beautiful Sins

this is written with a nod to the great Oscar Wilde - "beautiful sins, like beautiful things, are the privilege of the rich" & "in the consciousness of degradation" are from chapter 6 of "The Picture of Dorian Gray"

beautiful sins
from the mind they come
      [but appear as if from nowhere]
the roots of which running deeply
acute and blind

they need
they are searching because they know they
need

there is an intimacy with which they are
familiar and quietly ashamed
it's the depths they know
but not what lies beyond
it's the seeking they know
where sustenance runs like thick veins
waiting to relinquish

the tricks and pitfalls straddle the line

between obvious and obscure
the tricksters have their arrangements made
they have lures for all of us,
and the occasion to use them, you see,
dazzling and distracting and doing what
lures are supposed to do
they are reminders of all the things secretly
sought
precious and worthless
-here is the attraction presenting itself as
innocent
here is the suggestion that somehow
everything will be all right

the story is simple and easily remembered
it rolls off the tongue with the kind of
conviction no one would question

like beautiful things
these rich privileges provide adequate
temptation
      [no one is looking]

more than simply approachable
open enough, vulnerable enough
meaning as much as imagined
this depraved promise, its grinning maw

its glimmer of sanctuary
- in it, redemption is alluded to
>[no one is looking, you know what to do]

the satiation of hunger stands boldly and
sells itself shamelessly
-this is where decisions begin to accrue
where the importance of things germinate
new needs

this is where hope helps
where a vague sense of faith can be friend
and foe
here, in the instance known as sharing
here, in the consciousness of degradation

Remainders and Casualties

no way around
waiting to be pleased

anticipating what is next
wishing away what's left

pushing, pulling,
making any way at all toward an obvious
end

who made the rules and when?

each word falls
each is the casing of what was

so much refuse in a moment of need
too much need in the moment to refuse

the weight of it all accumulates
faster than comfort can accommodate

do we wait here or move on?
do we wait, too, for the reaction to fall?

each of our pieces stand alone

nothing fits the way you'd think
there is friction to take into account
there's all that's odd about each to consider

force is always an issue
it's always the consideration we deny

is it all so precious to not be the sacrifice?
is it all so precious?

Of Surface and Substance

the field is full
it looks full
it may even feel full

the edges have been reached
the limit of it set
approached
carefully considered

the inches of it
the square inches of it are filled
have been filled, they contain
they contain things that fill
they contain things to be described
to be seen
weighed
sometimes wanted
sometimes things to be discarded

there is a desire running through
there is a continuity
it makes sense to some
there is the surface and there is the
substance

it makes sense because you've been there
it makes sense because there is difference
because when discerning
the differences make themselves apparent
and the meaning of full starts to change
and for you
the meaning of full starts to change

Tasks and Tick-marks

sometimes clawing, sometimes clamoring
for attention
its grip is cool and quick, its voice, even with
a quiver, is never *less* demanding

it feels like a new task, but it is an old one
renewed
been around the block, I see, still not
simple, still not easy

or pretty, still with the energy and impact,
still with the qualities
and personality that makes it something to
fight shy of, something to face,

something to contemplate *again,* to try to
tuck neatly away
it fights the folding, it fights the creases, it
takes the effort as a compliment.

this is the list we all make at one time or
another, the note to self
reminders, good intentions, dirty little
secrets, the place where

the sorting can happen, where the edges of
things can be softened
because *you said so*, because it was noted as
such or meant to be

this is how categories come into being, how
reckoning grows to be important
with its tick-marks, with its mindless
scrawling leaking from the margins

into the body, darkening the doors of these
ideas and intentions
until what's left feels tattered again and soft
between forefinger and thumb.

In Development

not new, hanging like skins in layers loosely
forgiving the harshness of the details as they
are pressed into the apparent, making
images
that appear sweetly, the way images prefer
to be seen, the way they insist on being
                        remembered

here, in the darkness hanging
filling the space that the room is
the space between, where one ends
and the other begins
this feels like intimacy
      across the bed, across the bedding
      across the layers and folds
      across the arm outstretched
along the length of it
along the implied strength of it
      not reaching out to but still there
      not in action but still ready to act
      not only filling, to a certain degree
covering, the way water covers
the way it becomes a part of that with which
it interacts

here, the darkness hangs
in some places as if solid
as if not hanging at all, but standing
                          on duty
    to guard and cloak and cover
    to soften what the day left jagged
    to minimize, diminish and
dispurse in some places like veils
there to conceal, mask
leave to the imagination
the many wonders of which no one knows
how to speak
    to make for the mind
and therefore the soul?
a mystery out of the familiar
    to weave into this a sense of
eroticism
    to make for the senses other than
sight
a delight the light of day bleaches
and tends to makes bland

here, where the arm outstretched
feels like it *means* something
    where, with the slightest of
movement
the space between would begin to dwindle

        where the darkness would cover
and still fill but the shape of it
would be different than it once was
        this is when enough changes to be
noticeable
but not obvious
        this is when participation outweighs
observation
the touch of one being against the being of
another

here, hanging in the stillness
        in the darkness hanging
        in the layers as they are in relation to
themselves
the movement, as itself
and as the thing it is about to become,
makes itself known
makes the intention that transformed it
from impulse to action known
and then it becomes
and then there is the reaction to it
the impulse in return
the reaction half-heartedly predicted and
desperately hoped for

here, the darkness has done what it does

here, in the cover provided
in the forgiveness
the image, as it was, is no more
there is a matching of shapes
seemingly unrelated, there is the unchanged
volume but the arrangement's been altered

here, in the layers and folds
in the complexities
the darkness presses into being that which
is
as intangible as it is real

In Position

from the middle
there is the appearance or suggestion of
equidistance
if linear
if circular
      if logic dare bear or attempt to apply

from here
reaching but not taking into the hand
that for which the extending of the self was
initiated
like an exposure more than the intent itself
like a theory tried and retried and
adjusted to not only make due
but prove itself once and for all
beyond its bounds and definition

there are tenets regarding temptation
there are best efforts that fall flatly
there are series of things that can stand
alone but do not
there is the epiphany of identification
disguised as enlightenment
calling and moaning and begging to be
recognized

there is the place around which all of this
orbits and affects
an intermingling of gravities and influence
at times pushing away
at times pulling

despite this position
this choice
that found to be lacking is the story line
what could or should be is the plot and
what binds it into being isn't purpose or
intent or
the actions of those involved
but the sole fact that potential is the
outcome
waiting to be realized

The Result

she was old enough, older than most
in her there was experience and know-how
from the years, from the life lived
from the time elapsed that already felt like a
lifetime

starkly, in the light not so much flickering
but
cycling sixty times per second at a rate one
would think imperceptible, she heard the
words
saw them being formed, the doctor's lips dry
as they too (anxiously) cycled in and around
the letters coming together carefully
forming
syllables, then forming words then
becoming
the message delivered

there in the bright white, it all came
together
the delivery crashing and then the
deciphering
the words like signposts approaching -
cancer

and pregnant - choices and chances
there, starkly, not swimming but drowning
in the unrelenting glare of tools and
coils of things stacked and organized
and sterile

the words, like ruffians, ran rampant and
and tangled with the reality unfolding and
complicating things and making a decision
like a coin-toss into something more -
there are chances, there are choices

and of course the pause like a surprise
silently waiting, it too becoming part
of the moment and part of the complicating
of things
part of the deciphering and decision making
imploring, by its hollowness alone
the need to be filled

Balance

From the point of belief there is born
carried on, and from that point on
that which is one step further
          a tradition
On the surface of things
there is the tangible challenge -
 you know it like the truth, it feels like it
it makes the sense necessary to make proof
something of a bystander
to make logic and all the things that make it
     so feel like theory
         and happily so
I'd never thought about this day until it fell
into being
as if remarkable
     I wanted to
     It seemed like an eventual need
But it never presented, it never materialized
it never made for anyone the kind of
argument that
         if challenged, would stand
And from that point, standing but eyes cast
elsewhere
with the tradition or belief also cast
elsewhere

the contemplation, hands in pockets, shoes
shuffling
becomes something unto itself
becomes
in its consideration
the possibility of the next step to be taken
hanging in the balance
        hanging
From the outside, the hues of things seem
important
looking in, the shapes of things, the sizes
all that comprises appearance
        seem to have value
I'd never planned for this day until it fell
into being
it can become remarkable at any moment
    I wanted to
    It seemed like an eventual need
But it never presented, it never materialized
from the balance there was an effort made
but never the kind of argument that
        if challenged, would stand

Second Nature

from the edge
in the shade of a pin oak
with my back to the afternoon sun
the teeming was undeniable
it appeared high-frequency-like
not nervous really
without anxiety
but quivering
 pulsing   vibrating.

even as a kid
I knew the difference
between a lake and a pond
this was a pond for sure
- compact, condensed
and thick with the sort of things
that define it as such
- the plants, though firmly rooted
in the dark, tannic soil
reached the surface
unfurled proudly
the blossoms of which
opening every morning in the fresh warmth
          greeting
and as it slid across the sky

          following
the sun.

I always had my fishing pole
and little, yellow tackle box.

I didn't fancy myself an angler
but it seemed cover enough
to trespass without
the suspicion being empty-handed caused

on this day though,
I was transfixed by the magic on offer

the stew of tadpoles
some with stubby rear legs
ceaselessly wriggling
the blackness of them and their sheen

the water striders
gliding on infinite dimples
in the stillness of late June

and the bullfrogs
from their shady repose
croaking occasionally
a lazy reminder of where I stood.

Contrarian

the common ground provides not
familiarity but that which familiarity
possesses
the respite and ease of being where guarded
ways and guarded days
                                             if
remembered at all
make themselves known the way dreams
tend toas if from the ether an appearance is
made
and with that there is the scant recognition
attached and associated as if to something
too quickly passing

this is the likely territory of upbringing
of that which may have been experienced
simultaneously
but not necessarily together

                         as father and son?

the times, dates and places unchanged
but that contained therein, for some made
better
softened by years or enriched

by the wisdom allotted by experience
for some made worse
seeds planted in a soil too dry
too cold and barren of those things nature
needs to nurture

this *is* the common ground
shared but not shared alike
with its affable approach and undemanding
demeanor
always coaxing come-hither
always cooing coquettishly
this is the place where
despite the truth and the facts as they are
written
we find that we want to believe more than
we actually do
and that proof is based both on faith and
logic

so here, back to back
some, side to side
commonly contrarian to the core
the world and its wares passes
and in its passing
picks up, parades
then discards the ephemera used as cues

                used as clues
                used to describe and define
in hopes of
but not necessarily for any
and not necessarily for all

Evidence and Reasoning

it's not enough to know
to be known
to have knowledge
and even to have a grasp of the kind of
understanding
that lends to the intangible
a sense of insight and perspective

what is enough?

in the right hands, in skilled hands
digits and palms and mastery of
movement
momentum
and   manipulation
there is an awareness that no exertion takes
place
that through practice and ritual
or something innate and inexplicable
the thing upon which the hands are laid
the product, the end result
      at first glance
appears machine made
or conjured as if from thin air
but upon closer scrutiny

reveals things about itself
about its creator
about the hands
and their endeavor to create
glimpses of personality
offerings from the inside
those pieces protected
in fragments now portrayed
- and in the reading, in the interpretation of
the process and therefore the person
conclusions by inference are drawn

at the right time
by allotment or lottery
though impossible to plan for but easy to
accommodate
the investment
the years not only accumulated
but actually spent begin to make sense
begin to align themselves orderly and in a
way pleasing to the eye
and add up as if a vessel by droplets filled
                        but full nevertheless

at the right time
foreboding be damned
it comes spilling out

without grief or a feeling of loss
the high-point is reached *not the*
apogee
where by hand
the squareness has been softened
and by consequence, the harshness
and at that edge
that voluptuous lip
with the grace we all know and the beauty
we tend to attribute
it comes spilling out like a new beginning
         a redistribution, if you will
         the finding of its own level
         always referred to
         but now finally understood

To Be Expected

there are times when it feels like you are
waiting for an opponent
and there are times when it feels like he's
waiting for you

>in the forgotten places
>now neatly tucked away
>that place where *categories* are
important
>where boxes of other boxes of things
thought precious reside

>like matchboxes from a bar-fight
>keys to whatever
>good times won fairly
>and the bitter times softened
>by age and confabulation

is it always like this?
will it always be like this?
breaking and broken
promise not to tell?
the anger tastes like blood,
the joy, like life's sweetest reward

be it by trial
each move a calculation
deliberate and practiced
or by error
it feels as if everyday falls from the sky
as if the effort was never put in
or it was forgotten about entirely

    "balance happens" I tell myself
    then smile and walk away

Theory and Law

as the opening begins
as it becomes apparent that this is what it is
and that it is happening
the effort becomes a momentum
the reaction to the opening being just
behind
that which spawned the movement
          (*is this equal and opposite?*)

you see
first there is
and as if to prove itself
then there was
like steps taken
like a procedure unfolding
unaware of why
unaware of itself being a procedure
even as it unfolds
    (*"We have reached mastery when
we neither mistake nor hesitate in the
achievement"*[1])

this is where the overlap becomes

---

[1] Friedrich Nietzsche on mastery.

something significant

something recognizable

this is where one thing is met with another

where one thing meets

and in some cases

displaces the other

    proving a theory of matter

    following a law of physics

        (*"Every body perseveres in its state of being at rest or of moving uniformly straight ahead, except insofar as it is compelled to change its state by forces impressed"*[2])

---

[2] Cohen & Whitman 1999 translation of Isaac Newton's first law of motion.

Us or Them

technically, on the floor there
in the hierarchy we know as kingdom
in circles, running and running
it is not a who but more a what

at first light frozen
caught in whatever act that act could be

in the hunt for...
in the process of what the purpose should
be

over the first lip folded, into the dark again
into the unsuspecting
to shelter, to lay in wait
to hide maybe or escape more
than just the light
more than just what the light provides
to find that sense of safety, of real security

     under the foot fall falling
under the weight of it
under the end-all perceived but not learned

in the breaking of one into another

      the shadows into light
the light into being
the being up against the intent of the other

if not to protect, then what(?)
if not to extend one at the expense of
another, then what(?)

it is the many steps involved, from dark to
light

the hand on the switch to cover or fill one
with the other

the immediacy suggested by the Tungsten
reacting
resisting, glowing to near white but not
quite

the succession of thoughts that fulfill the
impulse
that is itself a reaction that is no longer
explained or explicable

and in that
the act itself, shallow and barbaric
a pittance lending definition to an irrational

reaction that
in turn illuminates the dead end of what
was

                              this is not pride or
proud
this is not the realm of bully-kings where
might is right
or where the vagaries of intelligence or
evolutionary chance
outweigh the respect that ought to be
universal but for some reason
in this situation every time is lost

this is the territory of the knee-jerk
of the cowardice-kingdom-come-crusader
out to outdo and in an instance
overcome the burden borne

as if a hero
as if with nothing to apologize for
but the wrong place and the wrong time

In Beijing

out into the absolute, shared like a badge of
honor
the busloads, the taxis taking to and from
people with flags leading those without
on loudspeakers, in too many languages and
irregular cadences

out into this thing referred to as a square
throngs, throngs of throngs
the place where if one were to break free
they'd be absorbed by another passing
passel
a constant stepping into and out of

here the sky is grey, the sun is held back
imprisoned by the grey
here, the only thing that could possibly
understand the scope of where
of why
of how it is we came into being
of how we came into being here
is itself restrained, controlled and in perfect
order

here we have scrutiny

for each of us there is another
another assignment, a thing to do and make
note of
here the observation need not make sense
any longer
it is so because someone said so

in the middle of what seems like forever
this shape with no boundary
this suggestion of a power so great that no
one dare question it
I found myself lost and lost again
filled with questions with no one to ask

within this boundless being there are places
where cues start
where with only one there begins an
amassing
from there it widens
and in doing so
begs to be kept in check
from there it snakes its way around and
back and forth

the millions here scuffling and shuffling
along
chatter and whir and together

they sound like a sickness of the inner ear
     - this is where orderly excitement is expertly contained
     - this feels like the birthplace of uniformity

Exchange

1

the story is told and retold
it is wound and rewound
it coils around itself
it is a story around a story
the telling of it
that which tightens the loose spots
makes up for the missing parts
acts as an anchor to the drifting that can
take place
          as it is assembled this
countless time
as it is formed from account and creation,
the words of it almost meaningless until
heard
          until gathered up and heard

2

what wants to be told
    - we wait because we have to
        brief abstractions so
believable it's true -
is everything

3
with the one side begging

not real begging

not on the knees of desperation

hands clasped as if before the lord

      but asking

wanting to hear and asking to be told

4
there is the story

there is the telling of it

5
the words woven into winter woes

into tales that make human nature feel like

something

like something new

something to believe in

because

at times this is all we have

6
into heroes born of necessity and

into the bleakness everyone dislikes but

is comfortable with

7
the yearning to be held
to be received and
accepted like a son
like a sibling
like the lover that once was
in the arms of the story waiting
in the embrace of the meaning implied

Tertiary

witnessed as if in a dream
the tree branch bending
a stooping
a load being born

      a spring being wound

under the weight itself
from the pushing off of
a reaction to the pushing off of

still to be seen
there is the resemblance
of an attack launched
of a departure from hiding on high

out of the periphery

into the now as it is briefly perceived
 into the zero second of reaction
      into the fight or flight

the canopy awash with the reds and yellows
of autumn
the fruit of a season's growth hanging heavy

hanging ripe and waiting
a feast for the songbirds flourishing
darting in and out
the darting of beaks breaking crimson beads
the quick consumption

itself a kind of departure

in a brash flash as I approach
the wings beating
the controlling of air
      the contortions of being
of a frenzied feeding
it is here, witnessed as if in a dream
the facing of and the back to the concept of
survival

and there in my approach
out of the periphery
the product of observation
the summary of limited learning
at terminal velocity incoming

in my pausing
I don't know if I should freeze
it feels as if I should scream
or do something, anything

and as quickly as it was noticed as a thing
beginning
it is the thing ending
a fierce finale - now nothing but feathers
falling
as beautiful as it is vulgar

Interim

1
like an uplifting
a thought in the rising
like smoke   like a specter

2
a leaf caught windswept
cavorts in the shadows
then flickers brightly in the shafts of light
        penetrating

3
like fingers extended
from the arms outstretched
a waiting embrace
        a stepping out of winter

4
here we have an
instance
that feels as if forever was
upon us

5
this is the pause meant to be taken

a child again, lost
> carefree

immersed in the depths of innocence

6

the first autumn to be remembered
> for some reason
> significant
> or otherwise
> tangible

7

the first time, as if from enchantment
gravity garnered meaning
had a sense to be made of it
made a show of itself

8

dappled and daring in red
fluttering, almost floating
flaunting its seraphic self
and there
a mid-air meeting
the fleeting thought greeting

grabbing this last dance to the ground

Null Set

impressing upon each other

the blind intent
the meaning of what we've reached

this place, this point
this perfect progress is a lending
                                      a leaning
      an end to the ambiguity

here the inaccuracies are hammered out
here we do not resemble ourselves

recognition is done
it was the first step
the first stop
that which began this process

we are then found
pressing, pushing, piercing
following the lead left by what was
identified
by what was recognized

in, on or near

what we have in the failed light

is shared if unseen
felt but still unsure

a reliance on proximity
where deeds and measures
are met and mended
coalesced beyond decision

here, all the middle distance is accounted for
here, the approximation nullifies the unlikeness

Ether

*held agog as if to say or in preparation to
refer to -*

in one
there is the power to transfix
to loosen from the bounds
that which has been staid
or attuned otherwise

there is the pent up and unspeakable which
not blossoming but bursting
creates immediately an atmosphere
at once of surreal surprise
and tangental escape.

in the other
fixed then transfixed
the uprooting routes and reroutes

as a sense is sought
as a clarification is coerced from the
collected
grappled with and then lost

in the other there is the passive

- observation, hesitation and the lacking reaction.

this is what it's like

engulfed by
overpowered by

restrained
 and at bay

Validation

in the air surrounding us
filling the space around us
between us
(the air is the space and the filling of the
space)
fitting into the incompleteness where
everything seems to fit together cleanly
but doesn't

in those spaces and
the spaces that connect them one to another

sometimes end to end
a comforting conformity
sometimes willy-nilly

through this conduit
formed by the area filled and
the areas assumed to be filledwave-like
ripples rounding each other

forming a succession
forming an insistence

that which (I think) is implied

the sound and the meaning of sound

the sound and its source make

if only momentarily

their presence known

this lets us know we're not alone

this lets us know we're still alive

      this lets us know

In Simple Acceptance

without spoken words
or the encumbrance of the words written
the placement is that of a mindless
searching
a reaching for and grasping of
the filling, if only for now,
that which (if only for now?)
feels the emptiest

taken into the hand,
the familiar hand of another
hand in hand

    - its warm embrace
    - its extension of one to another

still silent,
still without the words that mark as and
define thusly
here the outreach is acknowledged,
the notion reciprocated

without benefit or blessing
or requisite shame
this carrying forth of the idea that,

if unconsciously accustomed
this creature comfort,
instead of being bleak or blanched at
is something basic
not brazen,
something bearing
not barren

Seam

at the seam
where,
carefully trimmed,
edge matching edge
two, initially opposing
undergo and grow,
the needle's passing
through and through
a progression
a change - an enforcement

where the patterns
like choices
can stray
the intention,
the lofty premeditation
held to the highest
stands restrained
by passionless hands,
dim expectations
and stone-faced execution

at this end
hanging hangdog
another attempt

another shell

a departure point

really

reached and wrung

wrought

as if from hope

 as if from hope

Upheaval

it breaks
in a staggered moment
it breaks again

here
obviously radiating from somewhere
it makes its way from South to North
where and how it does
from time to time
varies
but the effect is the same

the swelling
taking its time
being of itself and own purpose
rising without notice
pushing toward its own inevitable rebound
and there
unstoppable
it breaks
sometimes with a crash
sometimes softly
with a whimper

Passing in the Fog

incremental in its exposure
if only at first

through the distance
itself an erosion

a brief recognition of color
blue and then red

through the refraction
carried softly by dim light

a sudden awareness of form
i think it's a man
and then the movement of the form

in this
this passing

there is a parsing of details
there is the passive restraint

the obstruction
and the moment when
as if necessary

a conclusion is drawn
and
without a word
there is the moving on

Turf

swaybacked landscape
a field of giving

under hand

under foot

begging to be entered
the sun warming

without witness

without words

Magnetism

the hush
by its existence
is drawing

there is a gravity to it
that can't be explained
a voice to it
that keens and beckons
or
mews softly like a mistress
for you to come
out into
or
nearer than you'd normally dare

the hush
with its insistence
is pulling

there is a magnitude to it
that just *is*
a certain facet of its many
that can't be ignored
or
left on its own

like a father to his child

a sense, really

or

that thing we refer to as instinct

the hush

with its sitting

and waiting

and perfect patience

will take you when ready

accept you when willing

hold you when nothing else can

4.56am

in the aubergine solitude
at the center of the hush

in this place known as mid-pause
where heartbeats thunder

the body trembles
at the thought of progress

When the Treetops Whistled

each broke like dawn
at dawn
when the winds peaked
responding to their warming

from where the table was
to its new resting
fallen - forced
on its side now - against a windbreak

the chairs too lifted
rearranged and disrupted
from where they sat opposite
across three votives collected

now in static rays
as the light breaking reveals
an assumed trajectory
and the evidence of impact

here amongst the wind-whipped
the only things found still
their shard sharp ends glimmering
both elegant and unfortunate

Opening of

in the time taken
or in the time invested
there should be

    in that

a balance that
in the least
discusses the position known as neutrality
and that of the side taken

so, both sides
and no side at all

in that
the place shared
is that
of the origin
where divergence is the key

the commonality
is that of a place
where an impetus partakes
of its opportunity

In the Welling

the wallows fill first
the shallows spill
and from the edges
dripping lazily
that which may be the excess
 or worse
obsolete

here
where the fluids mix
 and muddy
where from the stillness
sediments loosen in the colloid
a patterning bubbles and subsides
rises and again falls
that for a moment
a lending
to itself
and the entirety

Restoration

take my hand and
if you could
or rather
if you would
lead me away
lead me astray
and break for me
this that I cannot

my will, if you will
goes to great lengths
to appear as if impotent
yet wins all the arguments

and bullies   -   coerces

makes a mockery of control
take this too
in your hand
and make for me anew

find the edges
once there
find the rough spots
those places battered

those places that look the part of neglect

hone smooth
and please
for me
refine
in your grip
between your hands
under the pressure applied
and insisted upon

for me
patch the threadbare
shore the weak spots
piece the remnants
make whole
for me
what little there is left

Of Opportunity

repeatedly, but in no set order
no discernible pattern
from looking briefly
skimming through
      turning away.

each   glistening
is a reaching out
      or to
a doubling back
arching, as if into,
      or across

each   glistening
in the steep light provided
of such an afternoon

flexing and formation
flush with freedom
askew or akimbo
      (I cannot make a choice)
in a shimmering dance

each   glistening
along the shaft

at the tip
and follicular home

each   glistening
in the steep light provided.

If Only Slight

just as the embrace breaks
as the bodies,
in unison
make distance, re-make distance
where
for an instance
it had been displaced
replaced by a union of yearning
a filling of
until the very moment when
belly meets belly
and arms entwine
and retrieve each into the other

just as the embrace breaks
the arms open for another
seeking symmetry's comfort
an allotment of balance
the sort of fulfillment
provided by another
any other
as if, through time
their passing takes on meaning
supplicates a definition
becomes a constant

just as the embrace breaks
just as time becomes
the time you know to release
and into the world
set free
this glimmer of comfort
this being
being sweeter in return

and as the embrace breaks
it leaves in it's wake
a resonance, a reassurance
to quell the fear's rising
in the space where once,
however briefly
you held the being of another
and knew the reasons why you bother
why you bother at all

Of Scrutiny and Hindsight

the motion here is that of a changing
perspective
and that of a provisional offering
standing as if waiting to change
as if waiting to
change and be changed again
the light, from its fixed position
is a charity
a contribution that becomes apparent
as soon as it *becomes* light
an allowance that becomes important
long after it becomes apparent
this apparent clarity
is the gift hindsight provides
the shadows and the shapes of shadows
and the contours created
lend assistance to that which is assumed
to that which is yet to be seen
in this evolution of observation
as the body passes into,
through and beyond the light's reach

Man.1

it is the skin of him
at first
and at a distance
that does the talking
that tells a story
or at least imparts an intimation upon
what is for me
his first light.

nut-brown or as of dark wood
that which he chooses to offer
if not just for my perusal
then instead
for the whole world to witness
if for a moment anyone was to
in their passing
note privately, that, which I'm sure
is lacking the specific intent perceived
the very moment eyes, by chance, have the
pleasure
however briefly
to be filled by the boon of mere presence
that which, though not accidental
in itself is a portrayal.

he reads like a Hemingway
like the salt of the earth
like the grit in the teeth
of a hard day's work that rewards
a sort of satisfaction earned and effortlessly
shared as
in blithe repose
with thick-set arms folded
and resting atop his belly
rounded somewhat and pressing snugly
into a grey tee-shirt
he, in a conversation I can't quite hear
leans back and lets loose a deep
hearty laugh
that leaves me pleased
and perhaps a little hungry for more.

Denouement

there is an end of which we never speak

it can hold you, heal you
treat you like the child you become
because of it

it can feel like a need

the end exerts a dominance
asserts itself as ominous
pushes praises from a sour mouth

sits as a surprise, though we know it

this is the end that has no ending
no limits
the end that sits like a trap
waiting

a space waiting for its fill

the end lends itself willingly
to the thoughts that arise
when sleep fails
to the weighty power

of superstition

it stands like a warning

it is an answer never asked of
but always right
never addressed
but always right at home

this is the end without terms
and compromise
without "what if?"
or an inclination
to bargain

it happily holds the cards
stacks the deck
deals from the middle
with an arrogant grin
the end makes the days long with worry
the night is rife with the sense that
here in this place of powerlessness
the only hope remaining
is that of a better ending

As if Gossamer

1
still in the this

the afterglow
as it's known

the morning's visitation
as sudden as suggestion.

here,
the implications are just thoughts
 - fleeting, flitting and furtive.

their impact,
if any,
negligible
if measured against the moment
as it happens
as it happened

if compared
contrasted

if considered at all.

2
in these moments
intellectualism is forgotten
or not a requirement.

      instead, as animals
there is only the insistence of presence
of being
of involvement and instinct
force and acquiescence.

3
there is only that
which we intend to
create or construct and,
at the same rate,
deconstruct.

for this
if considered at all
is but a moment in the making.

www.ingramcontent.com/pod-product-compliance
Lightning Source LLC
Chambersburg PA
CBHW032149040426
42449CB00005B/453